Millenarianism: An Essay

Edwin David Sanborn

In the interest of creating a more extensive selection of rare historical book reprints, we have chosen to reproduce this title even though it may possibly have occasional imperfections such as missing and blurred pages, missing text, poor pictures, markings, dark backgrounds and other reproduction issues beyond our control. Because this work is culturally important, we have made it available as a part of our commitment to protecting, preserving and promoting the world's literature. Thank you for your understanding.

MILLENARIANISM:

AN ESSAY

READ TO THE

Pastoral Convention of New Hampshire,

JUNE 1855.

BY EDWIN D. SANBORN,

PROFESSOR IN DARTMOUTH COLLEGE.

PUBLISHED BY REQUEST OF THE CONVENTION.

Reprinted from the Bibliotheca Sacra for July, 1855.

ANDOVER:
PRINTED BY W. F. DRAPER.
1855.

Entered according to Act of Congress, in the year 1855, by
WARREN F. DRAPER,
in the Clerk's Office of the District Court of the District of Massachusetts.

MILLENARIANISM.

"Here," said a student to Casaubon, as they entered the old Hall of the Sorbonne, "is a building in which men have disputed for four hundred years." "And," asked Casaubon, "what has been settled?" How does it happen that the labors of learned men so often prove utterly worthless, and rather encumber than aid the honest inquirer after truth. It is simply because they mistake the proper objects of human inquiry, and exceed the limits which God has set to the understanding of man. They investigate subjects that cannot be known, and attempt to solve questions that cannot be answered. It is probable that one half, at least, of the works of philosophers and theologians might be annihilated, in a moment, without abridging the means of human improvement, or injuring the cause of true science. "Our public libraries," says Hallam, "are cemeteries of departed reputation; and the dust accumulating upon their untouched volumes speaks as forcibly as the grass that waves over the ruins of Babylon." Fortunate would it be for mankind, if the Babylon of controversial theology were sleeping, side by side, with its great prototype; but modern enthusiasts build again the tombs of the old prophets and those potent heresiarchs, who ruled among the nations, in former ages, "even all of them lie in glory, each in his own house." If their *tomes* were as innocuous as their *tombs*, we would "let the dead bury their dead," in quiet; but the literature which bewilders and misleads the humble inquirer after Divine truth, is infinitely more pernicious than that which caters to the passions of the carnal heart. There is hope that the "very chief of sinners" may be converted and saved; but the state of those fanatics, "whose little reading and less meditating, hold ever with hardest obstinacy that which they took up with easiest credulity," is truly desperate. Of all the books that have

"Escaped decay's effacing fingers,"

none are more worthless than commentaries on prophetic symbols. It is our honest conviction, that, if every theory and speculation, advanced by scheming theologians respecting the future history of the world, and based, as they pretend, upon the dark imagery of the Apocalypse and the book of Daniel, were obliterated from the minds of men, sound doctrine and true religion would be promoted. Do we, by this declaration, disparage the study of prophecy? By no means. The predictions of the Bible already fulfilled present a field of research broad enough and ample enough to employ the best thoughts both of men and angels who "desire to look into these things." Besides, "the pure word of prophecy" has other and higher uses and aims than merely to foretell future events. It has warnings for the thoughtless; reproofs for the erring; threatenings for the incorrigible; instruction for the ignorant, and consolation for the faithful. Contemplating, in the light of revelation, the history of the past, the stirring events of the present, and the "exceedingly great and precious promises" for the future, the devout student may well exclaim; "The works of the Lord are great, sought out of all them that have pleasure therein." To such topics let the curious mind confine itself, nor once attempt "to pry between the folded leaves" of God's secret book.

> "Beyond, abstain
> To ask, nor let thine own inventions hope
> Things not revealed, which the invisible King
> Only omniscient, hath suppressed in night,
> To none communicable in earth or heaven."

Certain great truths are so plainly revealed in prophecy, "that he may run that readeth." Among these we may class the ultimate triumph of Christianity, and the second advent of its founder. But *by what instrumentality will the church achieve its conquests?* and *for what purpose will our Lord come a second time?* The answer to these questions concerns our present duty, and every Christian should be fully persuaded, in his own mind, respecting them. The church of Christ, with great unanimity, in all ages, has taught that the world is to be converted "by the foolishness of preaching," accompanied by the Holy Ghost sent down from Heaven; and that the Saviour will appear a second time, not "to seek and save the lost," but to judge the quick and the dead. With the second advent of Christ, the end of all sublunary things and the final judgment of all men have been uniformly associated. In opposition to these views millenarians maintain: *

1. "That to spiritualize the symbolic prophecies is altogether wrong."
2. "That the slaughter of the two apocalyptic witnesses (Rev. xi.)

---

* Premium Essay by Rev. E. Winthrop, pp. 141, 170.

foreshows a real, literal slaughter of the faithful followers of Christ, represented — a slaughter which is yet future."

3. "That the anti-Christian powers are to be destroyed, not converted."

4. "There will be anterior to the millennium a real, literal resurrection of departed saints."

5. "The second coming of Christ will be before the millennium."

6. "There will be men living in the natural body on the earth after Christ's second coming."

7. "The millennium is to continue three hundred and sixty thousand years."

8. "A series of the most stupendous events is not very far distant."

Such is the outline of the new dispensation. Respecting the internal organization and social economy of this earthly kingdom, theorists vary indefinitely in their speculations. It would be impossible to state their doctrines to the satisfaction of all. They are as much at war with their own allies as with their antagonists.

"All, in their turn, accusers and accused;
Babel was never half so much confused."

Scores of commentaries on the unfulfilled prophecies have appeared within the last few years, from the elaborate treatise, in two bulky octavos, which grievously tax the time and patience of those who read, to the flying scroll written in rude hieroglyphics, and distributed, as a circular, by mail. The mental state of the writers is equally diversified, showing itself now in dispassionate sobriety and quiet mysticism, which often appeal to the best feelings of the Christian; now in the soaring rhetoric and terrific imagery of the heated partisan, causing the ignorant to tremble for the things that are about to come upon them; and now, in the enigmas of the confirmed lunatic who speaks in metaphors and writes in symbols. A collection of the fancy sketches of these dreamers and seers would form a body of romantic fiction which, in extravagance and absurdity, has no parallel in the annals of literature. The keystone of the whole system is the pre-millennial advent of the Saviour.

I. This doctrine, tested by the Scriptures, is, *in its principles*, doubtful and uncertain; *in its details*, impossible.

II. Tested by history, it is, in its infancy, an error; in its maturity, a heresy.

III. Tested by reason, it is absurd.

IV. Tested by the universal belief of the church, it is another Gospel.

V. Tested and known by its fruits, it is "evil only and that continually."

The interest which attaches to this theory depends, chiefly, upon *the time, mode and concomitants* of our Lord's second advent. If he is to come immediately, nay, if he is already advancing, so that the sound of his chariot wheels is heard by those who "*watch*" for his appearing; if the destruction of the anti-Christian nations and the conflagration of the "earth and the works that are therein," is at hand, "*at the very doors;*" then, it is in vain for Christians to labor for the conversion of the world and form plans having reference to a remote future. Viewed in this light, the subject assumes great practical importance; and the question of the pre-millennial or post-millennial advent of our Savior takes precedence of every other that can be presented to the present generation of men; for on it hangs the destiny of all the inhabitants of earth now living. Still the question cannot be answered by any party so as to silence objections and allay fears.

I. The nature of prophecy forbids it.

The time and mode of the fulfilment of predicted events are not revealed with sufficient certainty and definiteness to warrant the regulation of our present conduct with reference to them. God never designed to make prophecy a syllabus of history, so that men could resort to it as to the table of contents in a book, and read the important events of each succeeding year. The annals of past ages show, beyond a doubt, that neither the chronology nor the exact sequence of events were known to the most devoted students of revelation, until they actually occurred. Such prescience would interfere with man's free-agency, and reduce the Divine decrees to a blind fate. Hence those modern prophets who pretend to describe, beforehand, the marches and counter-marches of armies, the victories and defeats of particular monarchs, and the *exact* or even *proximate* date of the end of the world, like Ahimaaz of old, are running before they are sent. They are "swift witnesses," professing to foreknow what God has positively declared to be beyond the ken of men and angels. "The prophetic part of the word of God," says Robert Hall, "while it contains some general intimation of future events, is expressed in language or denoted by imagery proverbially obscure. This is intended to afford some general knowledge of the future, or it would not be prophecy; but, at the same time, obscurity forms a necessary ingredient. Were it free from that, were it like the language of narrative, it would give such a distinct knowledge of the future event as would lead some persons to use means for accomplishing it by their own power, and others presumptuously to frustrate it. The design of prophecy is not to enable persons to anticipate the minute circumstances of events, but partly to excite in their minds a general expectation, by presenting a vague and shadowy outline, partly, to afford a striking illustration of the power and providence of God in bringing to pass those events on the arrival of a distant age. The infinite wisdom of God appears in his foretelling future events in such a manner that, when they arrive, they tally and correspond to the prophecy, in a great variety of particulars; while, in the meantime, the events are so darkly shadowed that the human agents by whom they are accomplished are ignorant that in doing so, they are, in fact, fulfilling the counsels of Heaven. . . . Prophecy is not intended to give men such a knowledge of futurity as to enable the most sagacious to predict future events. Those who have attempted with certainty, to assign, beforehand, particular prophecies to particular events, have uniformly failed in their presumptuous endeavors. The design of prophecy is only to afford some general intimation which may operate either as warning or encouragement." If this view of prophecy be correct, those who attempt to define, exactly, *the time and mode and purposes* of our Lord's coming, have assumed false principles of interpretation, and are wrong in the essential elements of their theory. A large majority of the Old Testament prophecies have already been fulfilled. The record of their fulfilment shows that minute specifications of time, place, and circumstances could not have been made beforehand, even by the prophets themselves or the angels who " desired to look into these things." Nebuchadnezzar, Cyrus, the Assyrian king, Judas Iscariot and others all fulfilled the purposes of God, while they were pursuing their own selfish ends. With the prophetic biographies before them, the Jewish saints could not determine the time, place, and circumstances of their several actions, till their course was run. The destruction of particular nations and cities is described, in prophecy, with all the minuteness and accuracy of contemporaneous history; yet neither the prophets themselves nor those to whom their messages were delivered, knew *when or how* these events were to be accomplished. The first advent of the Saviour was announced in the very infancy of time; and, undoubtedly, there were good men who " waited for the consolation," in every generation; and some, perhaps, like their modern antitypes were every hour, during the whole four thousand years "*watching*" for the coming of the promised Messiah; but the result showed that they might have been better employed. The reason is obvious. The great plan of human redemption was announced, but the mode of its execution was concealed. The first gleam of hope dawned in Eden. In process of time the light increased; in the fulness of time, " the Sun of Righteousness rose, with healing in his beams." The first intimation of a Redeemer is contained in the declaration: "The seed of the woman shall bruise the serpent's head;" and the mother of all living, like many of her inquisitive children, thought the fulfilment of this prophecy *near at hand;* hence, she exclaimed, at the birth of her first-born; "I have gotten a man from the Lord." In this first announcement of a coming Saviour, there is no revelation even of his true character. It is not intimated that he should possess a Divine nature. The time and manner of his bruising the serpent are not foretold. Later in the world's history, Abraham receives the promise: "In thy seed shall all the nations of the earth be blessed." Those who in that age had a prurient curiosity to fathom the Divine counsels, without doubt, announced to the credulous that the world was on the eve of some great event. But here, the time, place, circumstances, and character of the blessing to be enjoyed are quite as obscurely shadowed forth as in the first promise. It is not even stated whether the blessings are to be temporal or spiritual, whether they shall proceed from *one* or *many,* whether human or Divine agents are to be the almoners of them. We pass down the stream of time to the age of Moses. He said to the waiting Israelites: "The Lord thy God shall raise up unto thee a prophet, from the midst of thee, of thy brethren, like unto me; unto him ye shall hearken." Now would it not be natural for the Jews to expect an exalted personage to succeed Moses as Lawgiver and Judge? The prophecy does not allude to the time of his advent, and only obscurely reveals his character. They could not certainly know, from the language of the prediction, that the expected prophet would be the Son of God. All that God saw fit to reveal to them was the fact of his coming; "the times and seasons he put in his own power." Further on, in the history of the Jewish race, we find other promises made to David of a successor who should sit upon his throne and rule the nations in equity — but the time and mode of that reign are still left in the dark. To Isaiah, brighter visions of Christ's future kingdom were disclosed. To him the divinity of the Messiah was fully revealed. "His name," says the prophet, "shall be called Wonderful, Counsellor, the mighty God, the everlasting Father, the Prince of Peace." Isaiah defines, more fully than any other seer, the various offices of Christ as prophet, priest, and king; still the time of his advent is not clearly revealed. Jeremiah and Ezekiel in their extended prophecies do not often allude to the expected Messiah. The passages which are supposed to refer to his future kingdom are obscure and difficult of interpretation. The minor prophets speak often of the promised Saviour and of the glories of his kingdom; but always in figurative or symbolic language. The terms by which the Saviour is designated by the prophets, are of uncertain import, till the light of history shines upon them. He is called "Shiloh," "my Servant," "a King," "the Root and Offspring of David," "the Prince of Peace," "the Branch," "the Desire of all Nations," and other appellations of kindred signification, all of which require elucidation to render them intelligible. The revelation of new truth gave new meaning to the words employed. The prophets were limited in their communications, by the language they used and the knowledge of the people they addressed. Had they introduced an entirely new terminology, and, by way of prolepsis, discoursed like a modern exegete, the people would have charged them with insanity. Had they departed widely from the *usus loquendi* of their age, they would have rendered their messages unintelligible, and thus have defeated the very object of their mission. They expressed themselves in the forms of religious thought then prevalent, and their revelation was consonant with the national belief. They addressed Jews; they were educated as Jews; consequently they inculcated the Jewish religion; they reverenced the Jewish law; they spoke the Jewish tongue, and clothed their thoughts in a Jewish dress. They did not contemplate even the abolition of the Jewish ritual. Jerusalem, in the future and glorious reign of the Messiah, would still be the centre of light and the dwelling-place of the great King. The temple, as of old, would be the abode of the Shekinah; and its service would become more grand and imposing. Zion would become "an eternal excellency, the joy of many generations." David's reign had been the most illustrious in their past history; he is, therefore, selected as the representative of their future deliverer to whom the gentiles would become tributary. His enemies will be the enemies of the coming theocracy; in a word, Judaism was to be regenerated; its religion revived, and its political and ecclesiastical power greatly extended. "The evangelical prophet," as he has been called, by way of eminence, did not, for a moment, contemplate the abolition of the Jewish ceremonial law or the forms of worship peculiar to his nation. In rapt vision he saw the universal spread of his own religion. "And it shall come to pass in the last days [an undefined future,] that the mountain of the Lord's house [Jehovah's temple] shall be established in the top of the mountains, and shall be exalted above the hills, and all nations shall flow unto it." All the prophets expected a prince to sit on the throne of David, a warrior to subdue the enemies of their nation, a conqueror to receive the homage and tribute of kings and to be himself "King of kings and Lord of lords." A literal interpretation of their language involves all this, and requires the Messiah to be, like David, "a man of blood," extending his dominion by the sword, and reigning, in earthly splendor, at Jerusalem, the capital of the world. It also requires the restoration of the priesthood of Aaron, the ceremonial law of Moses, and the first dispensation with all its imperfections. We are shut up to this, if we refuse to give a spiritual meaning to prophetic language. The ablest advocates of millenarianism admit this. We will quote a few authorities. Mr. Fry (Rector of Desford) says: "Zion and Jerusalem are to be the great source of spiritual blessedness to the whole world. This 'city of Jehovah' is represented as the grand centre and emporium of civil and religious power, whither all nations resort for their laws and government. 'He shall reign in Jerusalem unto the ends of the earth.' . . . But what most surprises us is, that a ritual worship, so like the Mosaic ceremonial, should again be restored by Divine appointment, rather than institutions more analogous to the Gospel church; and especially that the *sacrifices of animal victims* should be again enjoined! For we read of all the various offerings of the Levitical economy, not only 'peace offerings' and 'meat offerings,' but 'burnt offerings,' 'trespass offerings' and 'sin offerings.'" "In Ezek. 43: 26," says Mr. Freemantle, "it is commanded that the priests shall purge the altar seven days. . . . And upon the eighth day and so forward, the priests shall make the burnt offerings upon the altar and God will accept them, thus *the legal ceremonies* will be celebrated upon the day of the resurrection of Christ. . . . Then the song of thanksgiving in Ps. lxvi. shall resound through the *temple aisle*. . . . 'We will go into thy house with *burnt offerings;* I will offer unto thee *burnt sacrifices of fatlings* with *the incense of rams;* I will offer *bullocks* with *goats.*' And this forms the fourth and last feature [of Israel's glory after the advent], viz. *the renewal of sacrificial worship.*" "At that [millennial] time," says Mr. Brock, "the [civil or political] *ascendency* of Israel will be paramount over the Gentiles. Clear to this effect are the predictions of the prophets." . . . "The same *ascendency* shall be exercised by Israel over the Gentiles *in spiritual things.*" "Jerusalem," says Mr. Pym, "shall be the METROPOLIS OF THE WORLD, *from which the law shall go forth* AND BE THE CENTRE OF WORSHIP FOR THE WHOLE EARTH. . . . God's people shall be exalted above all others." Mr. H. Bonar exclaims: "Why should not *the temple, the worship, the rites, the sacrifices* be allowed to point to the Lamb that was slain, in the millennial age, if such be the purpose of the Father? How *needful* will [such] retrospection then be to Israel! How needful when dwelling in the triumphant blaze of a Messiah's glory, to have ever before them some memorial of the cross, *some palpable record of the humbled Jesus*, some visible exposition of his *sin-bearing* work, in virtue of which they have been forgiven and saved and loved!"* How sensuous! how low, creeping and revolt-

---

* Quoted by Rev. David Brown, "Christ's Second Coming," p. 360.

ing to the Christian heart are such literal versions of prophetic language! The closing words of Zechariah, who is oftener quoted by millenarians than any other prophet, are these: "Yea, every pot in Jerusalem and in Judah shall be holiness unto the Lord of hosts; and all they that sacrifice shall come and take of them, and seethe therein; and in that day there shall be no more the Canaanite in the house of the Lord of hosts." If we must interpret this literally of the New Jerusalem, how great the change that awaits God's people to pass from the worship of their Saviour, "in spirit and in truth," to the slaughtering and offering of "slain beasts!" How marvellous is this retrogression from Christianity to Judaism! Is it not possible that the saints themselves, like the Israelites of old, may desire "to turn back" from this promised land, and thus give occasion to the great apostasy near the close of the millennium? It certainly shows great Christian self-denial in the venerable Dr. Cumming to be willing to exchange the warm precincts of Exeter Hall and the grateful homage of five thousand hearers hanging with rapt attention upon his "Apocalyptic Sketches," for the outer court of the temple and the pantomimic service of seething a piece of meat in a brazen pot. Verily, the Apostle Paul was mistaken when he said: "The law, having a shadow of good things to come and not the very image of the things, can never, with those sacrifices which they offered, year by year, continually, make the comers thereunto perfect." According to the modern view, those sacrifices not only make men perfect, but are "*needful*" to keep them so! If a literal version of the Messianic prophecies be insisted on, the Jews were right in their rejection of the Saviour. Christ has not yet come; Christianity is a fable; the Gospel, a mythology of "the Prince of Peace," must be given up for an exterminating warrior; for there is but one advent of the Redeemer, as King and Conqueror, spoken of in the Old Testament. A second advent would never be suggested to any reader of the prophetic Scriptures, who had not a theory to support. The second coming of Christ as the "Judge of the quick and dead" is obscurely revealed in the Old Testament, and clearly taught in the New. If the nations of the earth are to be given to Christ only that he may "dash them in pieces as a potter's vessel;" if, as Dr. Cumming thinks, "the kingdom of the Most High is about to crush and destroy all others, and the stone cut out without hands, i. e. Christ, is now actually falling upon those kingdoms, splitting them to atoms and scattering them as chaff is driven and scattered upon the summer threshing floor;" if, as Rev. Mr. Winthrop affirms, it is evident that the anti-Christian powers are to be *destroyed*, not *converted;* then, the Saviour we worship, who "did not strive nor cry," "who knew no violence," who was "holy, harmless and undefiled," is not the earthly conqueror predicted in the Old Testament.

It is in vain to say that Christ is "turning and overturning" the nations by his providence; for the world has always been so ruled and restrained, and such a plea does not answer the demands of a literal version of the prophecies. The truth is, a literal version is *impossible*. The millenarians uniformly themselves resort to a figurative, typical or symbolic meaning of a passage whenever the exigencies of their theory require it. It will be sufficient here to mention a few of the details of their system which involve physical impossibilities. Prophecy speaks of the Gentile nations going up to Jerusalem "from year to year," and "from one new moon to another," yea, "from one Sabbath to another." Jerusalem, if "all nations should flow unto it," could not contain them, not even if they were packed like mummies, in a solid mass rising a mile in height. Even if they should worship by proxy, and send "deputies," as is preposterously maintained by some, the time mentioned would not be sufficient for the going and returning. Besides, who can believe that those devout worshippers will not wish to go to court themselves and see the King of kings with their own eyes? If pilgrimages should prove as corrupting as they have been in the present world, it would not be strange if this *sauntering*, i. e. visiting "*la sainte terre*," should furnish additional grounds for the final millennial apostasy. The Jews and pre-millennialists both agree that the prophecies relating to the Messiah's kingdom remain to be fulfilled; that Jesus does not yet occupy the throne of David, and that his kingdom is yet future. "The Jews," says Mr. Brooks, "understood them [the prophecies relating to the kingdom] in their *appropriate and harmonious sense*, though not perhaps in their *full* sense; and the wonder is, *not that they should have thus understood them, but that any among ourselves should understand them otherwise*; seeing *that their primary and most obvious sense is so plainly accordant with the Jewish expectations.*" If the prophets describe a literal conqueror, they cannot possibly be understood to describe his literal foes. Isaiah says: "But they shall fly upon the shoulders of the Philistines toward the west; they shall spoil them of the east together: they shall lay their hand upon Edom and Moab; and the children of Ammon shall obey them." Now history and prophecy both agree in asserting the utter extermination of the nations mentioned in the above quotation. If a solitary representative of them still exists, it is not known to any modern ethnologist. If it be only the shades of departed nations that are to be mustered at Armageddon, the result will not be so appalling to human feelings as was anticipated. The New Jerusalem will then resemble the Indian's paradise. The Spectator informs us that an Indian Maraton went to the land of shadows—the Indian Elysium—to visit his deceased wife Garatilda. He found it surrounded by a seemingly impenetrable thicket of thorn-bushes; and for a time was at a loss what to do; but he soon found that it was only the ghost of a departed thicket, the shadows of thorn-bushes, and he walked through without difficulty. And what will the literalists do with such passages as these: "Even my servant David shall feed them;" "My servant David shall be a prince among them;" "David my servant shall be king over them;" "My servant David shall be their prince forever?" It would be a mere evasion of the literal meaning of these texts, to affirm that David will be an assessor with all the glorified saints who live and *reign* with Christ during the millennium. But the limits of a single Article will not permit us to pursue this topic further. We pass to the second proposition.

II. The doctrine of the pre-millennial advent of Christ, tested by history, is, in its origin, an error; in its maturity, a heresy.

It is admitted by psychologists that the mind, when engrossed by the contemplation of a single subject, becomes disqualified for the discovery or appreciation of truth. Everything is excluded but the solitary theme of interest. No light shines upon the mind's eye except that which is reflected from the minute focus of its own thoughts. Empirics avail themselves of this principle to impose upon the credulous by their specious wonders. Men are hypnotized, mesmerized, rendered insensible to pain, and cured of diseases, by arresting the attention and confining it to a single object. "Men of one idea" live in a perpetual state of somnambulism. A man who is committed to a theory is not a safe investigator of truth. It matters not how learned or devout the man of "peculiar views" may be; for in such circumstances the smallest portion of truth suffices so to engage the attention of men of superior intellect that they forget everything else, and become blind to all that is not comprised within the narrow circle of their own ideas. The theorist, like the spider, lives within the attenuated and feeble tissue which his own brain has woven. History becomes an excellent "alterative" for such a mental diathesis. "The raw and blustering polemic," says a competent critic, "who mistakes every reproduction of exploded heresies for something original with himself or peculiar to his own church, is very apt to sneer at the only pursuits which could have taught him better; and the self-inspired prophet or interpreter of prophecy, as well as the transcendental dreamer and declaimer, may be pardoned for their natural antipathy to history, as the science of facts and actual events." And what does history teach respecting the doctrine we are now discussing? It plainly and unequivocally affirms that it originated with the Jews and Judaizing Christians; that it was a part of the false and exaggerated notions of the Jews respecting their Messiah; that it was earthly and sensual in its character, and always productive of licentiousness and fanaticism. Philo, the Alexandrian Jew, expresses the conviction that the Mosaic law, the temple and the temple service, are designed for perpetuity. The Jews would be restored to their own country, and a golden age would begin from Jerusalem. Such was the "tradition" of the scribes and pharisees; so modern millenarians believe. "There was an old tradition," says the learned Kennicott, "alike common among Judaeans and Christians, sprung from the mystic interpretation of creation in six days, that the duration of the earth would be six thousand years; that the Messianic advent should be in the sixth millennium, because he would come *in the latter days.*" The Jews, therefore, made it an argument against the Saviour that his birth occurred too early in the world's history to answer the terms of prediction. "Many" [of the early Christians], says Neander, "seized hold of an image passed over to them from the Jews, and which seemed to adapt itself to their present situation, — *the idea of a millennial reign,* — which the Messiah was to set up on earth, at the end of the whole earthly course of the world, where all the righteous of all times should live together in holy communion. As the world had been created in six days; and, according to Ps. 90: 4, "a thousand years, in the sight of God, are as one day," so the world was to continue in its hitherto condition for six thousand years, and end with a thousand years of blessed rest, corresponding to the Sabbath. . . . The crass images, too, under which the earthly Jewish mind had depicted to itself the blessings of the millennial reign, had, in part, passed over to Christians. Phrygia, the natural home of a sensual, enthusiastic religious spirit, was inclined to the diffusion of this grossly conceived Chiliasm." Papias, bishop of Hierapolis, published many strange traditions respecting the physical pleasures to be enjoyed during the thousand years of Christ's earthly reign. He also records many miracles of the apostolic times which are not mentioned in the New Testament. Eusebius denominates him a man of limited endowments, and of unlimited credulity. "The injurious consequence of all this was, to foster among Christians the taste for a gross sensual happiness, incompatible with the spirit of the Gospel, and to give birth, among educated heathens, to many a prejudice against Christianity." "From what we have just said," adds Neander, "it is not to be understood, as if Chiliasm had ever formed a part of the general creed of the church." This is the highest authority for accuracy and impartiality which can be cited. This author uniformly represents millenarianism as a heresy attended with the gross ideas of a Mohammedan heaven. In discussing the doctrines of the Ebionites, he says : — " We must distinguish certain elements, possessing some affinity with Ebionitism, but involving a grossly material view of Christianity, since they adhered to *the sensuous envelope of the letter*, and failed of penetrating to its spirit, in affinity with the Jewish notion, which betrayed itself, for example, in the anthropomorphism and the anthropopathism of the doctrine concerning God; in the low, worldly views of the kingdom to be founded by Christ on earth; in *Chiliasm*." He regards the heresiarch Cerinthus as a connecting link between the Judaizing and Gnostic sects. He, in common with many of the Jewish theologians, expected "a happy period of a thousand years, when Jesus, having triumphed through the power of the heavenly Christ united with him, over every enemy, would reign in the glorified Jerusalem, the central point of the glorified earth." Eusebius says of him (we quote from a Latin version): — "Quippe hanc Cerinthi opinionem fuisse; regnum Christi terrenum futurum: et in iis maxime rebus quas ipse utpote carnalis et voluptatibus corporis deditus praecipue concupiscebat, haesurum: in ventris scilicet, et eorum quae sub ventre sunt satiatae; id est, in cibis ac poculis, in nuptiis et in iis quibus ista honestius parari posse, existimabat; festis nimirum et sacrificiis et hostiarum mactationibus." Near the close of the second century, Montanus arose in Phrygia, claiming to be a prophet of God, and announcing the immediate judgments of Heaven on the persecutors of the church, the second coming of Christ, and the approach of the millennial reign, whose happiness he set forth in the most glowing colors. He was attended by two prophetesses, named Priscilla and Maximilla. The latter declared expressly: "After me, no other prophetess shall arise, but the end shall come; in which, for once, she undoubtedly spoke the truth by mistake. "Scenes," says Neander, "somewhat akin to what occurred in Pagan divination, phenomena like the magnetic and somnambulist appearances occasionally presented in the Pagan cultus, were mixed in with the excitement of Christian feelings. Those Christian females, who were thrown into ecstatic trances during the time of public worship, were not only consulted about remedies for bodily diseases, but also plied with questions concerning the invisible world. In Tertullian's time, there was one at Carthage, who in her states of ecstasy, imagined herself to be in the society of Christ and of angels." How strangely do the aberrations of the human mind repeat themselves! But they grow more harmless, at each successive revolution; and we may, therefore, hope that, like those of the planetary system, they will ultimately correct themselves. "There is no subject," says Fontenelle, "on which men ever come to form a reasonable opinion, till they have exhausted all the absurd views which it is possible to take of it. What follies should we not be repeating at this day, if we had not been anticipated in so many of them by ancient philosophers and theologians. It has been maintained by some writers, contrary to the opinions of Neander above-quoted, that the belief in the immediate advent of Christ was universal among the early Christians. Admit that it was so; they were evidently mistaken; for in the time of the apostles he was expected to come during the life-time of that generation, but he did not so come. Then the expected advent was from age to age carried forward, till, wearied with mere conjecture and repeated disappointment, this fanciful theory was allowed to sleep. The general prevalence of such a notion rather makes against the arguments of modern pre-millennialists; for the more wide-spread the error the greater was the delusion. Gibbon says: "The ancient and popular doctrine of the millennium was intimately associated with the second coming of Christ, which was universally believed to be *near at hand*. As the works of creation had been finished in six days, their duration, in their present state, according to a tradition attributed to the prophet Elijah, was fixed to six thousand years. By the same analogy it was inferred that this long period of labor and contention, which was now almost elapsed, would be succeeded by a joyful Sabbath of a thousand years; and that Christ, with the triumphant band of the saints and of the elect, who had escaped death, or who had been miraculously revived, would reign upon the earth till the time appointed for the last and general resurrection." The Christians of the first century thought themselves living at the very dawn of a brighter era, and read the speedy dissolution of the earth, that then was, in "the signs of the times." Some Christians of the nineteenth century entertain precisely the same views, repeat the same arguments, observe the same "signs of the times," and are the unconscious victims of the same delusion. Dr. Cumming says: "On the supposition that the Jewish idea was a right one, that as there are six days in a week and the seventh is the Sabbath, so there will be six millennaries or periods of a thousand years, in the lapse of time, and the seventh will be the millennium. . . . We are now on the very dawn of the world's Sabbath!" Was ever sophistry more shallow? A Jewish tradition, originating no one knows where or when, based on a shadowy "*analogy*," which is unsubstantial as a dream, is made the foundation of a doctrine which is to regulate the practical affairs of this life, and to determine man's destiny for eternity! Can the "spiritualists" exceed this? In the creed of the English church, as it was first framed, says Milman, this view of the millennium was called "a fable of Jewish dotage," and rightly was it christened. The apocryphal gospels and spurious writings of the Jews abounded in allusions to the millennium. Gieseler informs us that "it was represented as a great Sabbath, which was very soon to begin, and to be ushered in by the resurrection of the dead. Till then, the souls of the dead were to be kept in the world below, and the opinion that souls were taken up into heaven before the resurrection, was considered a Gnostic heresy. The fancied enjoyments of the millennium were, in a high degree sensual and earthly." Jerome, one of the most learned and devout of the early fathers, says: "Apocalypsin Johannis si juxta literam accepimus, judaizandum est; si spiritualiter, ut scripta est, disserimus multorum Veterum videbimur opinioni contraire." Of the Latin fathers who advocated the sensuous views of the millennium which he opposed, he mentions Tertullian, Victorinus, and Lactantius; of the Greeks he mentions only Irenaeus, against whom he adds: " Dionysius, vir eloquentissimus, Alexandriae Pontifex, elegantem scribit librum irridens mille annorem *fabulam*, et auream atque gemmatam, in terris, Jerusalem, instaurationem templi hostiarum sanguinem, otium Sabbathi, circumcisionis injuriam, nuptias, partus, liberorum educationem, epularum delitias et cunctarum gentium servitutem." This enumeration of particulars shows what the early Christians expected; for the fathers whom he controverts are the most respectable advocates of the pre-millennial theory. In conclusion he says: " Quibus non invideo, si tantum amant terram, ut in regno Christi terrena desíderent et post ciborum abundantiam, gulaeque ac ventris ingluviem, et ea quae sub ventre sunt, quaerant." Epiphanius argues against the same carnal views, and asks with great propriety: " Quorsum igitur ab Apostolo dictum est: Si circumcidamini, Christus nihil vobis proderit?" Respecting the happiness of the glorified saints, he adds: " Quae oculus non vidit, nec auris audiit, neque in cor hominis ascenderunt quae praepararit Deus diligentibus se." Augustine, who certainly ranks as high with reference to his orthodoxy as any ancient father, says: " Quae opinio esset utcunque tolerabilis, si aliquae delitiae *spirituales* in illo Sabbatho affuturae sanctis per Domini praesentiam crederentur. Nam etiam nos hoc opinati fuimus aliquando. Sed cum eos qui tunc resurrexerint, dicant *immoderatissimis carnalibus epulis* vacaturos, in quibus cibus sit tantus ac potus ut non solum nullam modestiam teneant, sed modum quoque ipsius incredulitatis excedant; nullo modo ista possunt nisi a carnalibus credi." This is very strong language, uttered by one who knew that whereof he affirmed; and deliberately, soberly and truthfully he ascribes to the millenarians *incredible* licentiousness of opinion. Among the delights of Christ's earthly reign, Tertullian, the champion of ancient millenarians, mentions the following: " per eosdem mille annos infinitam multitudinem generabunt." It is not strange that the Mormons are staunch advocates of Tertullian's views. They have gone so far as to estimate the number of acres of land which will be assigned to each saint during the millennium. This is quite as rational as the fanciful notions above referred to. The doctrine under discussion, according to friends and foes, fell into disrepute on account of the extravagant notions entertained concerning it by its advocates. It is also worthy of notice that whenever it has been revived, it has ever borne the same bitter fruit. Dr. Hopkins, in his treatise on the millennium, says: "In the first three centuries after the apostles, the doctrine of the millennium was believed and taught; but so many unworthy and absurd things were by some advanced concerning it, that it afterwards fell into discredit, and was opposed, or passed over in silence, by most, until the reformation from popery. And then, a number of enthusiasts advanced so many unscriptural and ridiculous notions concerning it, and made such a bad improvement of it, that many, if not most, of the orthodox, in opposing them, were led to disbelieve and oppose the doctrine in general; or to say little or nothing in favor of the doctrine in any sense or view." Bishop Newton, himself a moderate advocate of the theory, says: "Some, both Jewish and Christian writers, have debased it with a mixture of fables: they have described the kingdom more like a sensual than a spiritual kingdom, and thereby have not only exposed themselves but (what is infinitely worse) the doctrine itself to contempt and ridicule." The notion of an earthly and temporal kingdom prevailed while the church was depressed and persecuted. When injustice triumphs in this life, the human mind instinctively looks to the future world for the vindication of the right. Here the belief in a judgment to come has its strongest hold of the conscience. Both the injured and the injurer, in their inmost souls, expect a righteous retribution. It was natural, therefore, that a down-trodden church should cleave to the opinion that Christ would "avenge his own elect," in person, on the earth where they suffered. But when Christianity became the predominant religion of the Roman empire, the doctrine lost its interest for the multitude and ceased to attract attention. It fell into general oblivion, because

III. Tested by reason, it was absurd.

It did not and cannot commend itself to the sober understandings of men. The new dispensation is essentially miraculous, as all pre-millennialists maintain. Its economy is, therefore, above the finite reason. Its administration is *supernatural*. All earthly analogies fail to represent it. The second person of the Holy Trinity reigns in person. Mortals know nothing of such a government. The saints have spiritual bodies. Of these we can form no just notions. Their mode of intercourse with the mortal races then living must be entirely conjectural. The common occupation of the renewed earth by mortal and immortal races is utterly unintelligible. We have no data, no experience, no history from which we can determine the power of the reigning class or the subjection of the subject class. From all that can be known of God, both from his works and word, sages and saints have inferred that he works by the simplest laws. Simplicity and uniformity characterize the laws of nature. Analogy would lead us to expect the same in the spiritual world; but in the hypotheses of pre-millennialists, we meet with *complexity* and *diversity*. The whole economy of redemption is converted into a series of experiments, instead of a perfect system, gradually unfolding as the race improved in knowledge, and thus "shining more and more until the perfect day." It seems strange to the uninitiated, that Christianity should be established on earth at such an expense of toil and suffering, only to result in a "failure" and be succeeded by a miraculous dispensation, which will also terminate in a general apostasy. It seems strange that Baptism and the Lord's Supper should be abolished, and circumcision and bloody sacrifices restored. It seems strange that the Bible and ordinary means of grace should be superseded, while men still live in the flesh and are still tainted with original sin, and give place to a new revelation. Rev. Mr. Bickersteth says: "There are some original and valuable remarks on the millennium, in the essays of Rev. H. Woodward. He shows *how inapplicable the Scriptures of the New Testament, written for a tempted and suffering church, are to this state of things.*" Dr. M'Neile says: "It is obvious that, in the passage from our present state to a state of universal holiness, THESE CHARACTERISTIC SAYINGS OF THE NEW TESTAMENT MUST CEASE TO HAVE ANY APPLICATION AND BECOME OBSOLETE, NOT TO SAY FALSE." It seems that Paul, in his elaborate argument to the Hebrews, to prove the imperfection of the old covenant, did not once allude to its ultimate restoration. It seems strange that it should be subjected to a temporary rejection of eighteen hundred and sixty-six years, and then be revived, in greater glory, for three hundred and sixty thousand years. It seems strange, too, that the blessed Saviour, when he wept over Jerusalem, did not offer one word of consolation to his afflicted people, by pointing them to its future glories. We have always believed that heaven is a *place*, not a state of the feelings or emotions. In heaven God is more immediately present, and holy intelligences pay to Him their unceasing homage. It is the place of which David speaks when he says: "In thy presence is fulness of joy and at thy right hand are pleasures forevermore." The inspired monarch evidently expected to spend his eternity there. Paul desired "to depart and be with Christ." He did not say, I desire that Christ may come and be with me. But where was Christ at the time Paul made this declaration? Before his ascension he said: "I ascend to my

Father and your Father." Paul says: "But this man, after he had offered one sacrifice for sins, *forever* sat down on the right hand of God." Could Paul have contemplated the cessation of Christ's intercession, during the larger portion of the existence of men upon our earth, when he says: "he *ever* liveth to make intercession for them?" Stephen, when about to exchange worlds, said: "I see the heavens opened and the Son of man standing on the right hand of God;" and dying, he prayed: "Lord Jesus, receive my spirit." The Scriptures teach that Christ came down from heaven, and after his resurrection ascended up where he was before. The righteous dead are undoubtedly with him in heaven. The Revelator says of those "who had come up out of great tribulation," "therefore they are before the throne of God and serve him day and night in his temple, and he that sitteth on the throne shall dwell among them." If this be so, the notion of an intermediate state so generally entertained by millenarians, must be a mere figment of the imagination. But if the glorified dead are now in heaven, why should a new residence be assigned them after the resurrection of their bodies? After enjoying the society of angels and dwelling in the presence of the "King of kings" for ages, will they be compelled to return again to earth and be forever separated from the companionship of holy beings who have never sinned? Is heaven to be unpeopled? Will the Father dwell alone for a whole eternity *a parte post?* Do the holy angels, who come with Christ, constitute the whole heavenly host? And is the Son to be forever separated from the Father and Holy Spirit? It has ever been considered an act of unspeakable condescension in him to leave "the glory which he had with the Father before the world was," and assume the human form. Why, then, when his work on earth is "finished," and he is restored to the bosom of the Father, should it be necessary for him again to return to the scene of his humiliation and sufferings? But admit that he will return to reign in Jerusalem, do we know the exact time of his advent? Do we know it with sufficient certainty to affirm that it is "*at the very doors?*" Such a supposition runs counter to the whole current of prophecy. It may be doubted whether a single prediction can be cited whose time of fulfilment was accurately determined beforehand. The fall of Babylon was foretold with a clearness and fulness which time converted into history. But it was a populous city for centuries after Isaiah predicted its utter destruction. The same is true of other cities and nations, whose ruins to this day bear eloquent testimony to the Divine prescience and veracity. Where definite numbers are used to indicate the duration of coming judgments, the full period was rarely completed with mathematical exactness. Nothing is more common in prophecy, than for a definite number to be used for an indefinite, or for a round and full sum of years to be employed to represent an approximation to it. Is the end of the age an exception to the whole tenor of prophecy? If so, why have the most sagacious critics so often mistaken the time? Why have dates been set, like mile-stones, all along the highway of time, to indicate the end of the world and its guilty inhabitants, and yet men still live and the world still rolls on? Why do honest and learned interpreters of the prophecies relating to this subject, differ from each other by thousands of years, if the meaning is plain? The Christians of the first century, misinterpreting the declarations of Christ respecting the destruction of Jerusalem, expected "the end of the age" and the new kingdom during their lifetime. Certainly, the Thessalonians, who were persuaded by visionary teachers that "the day of Christ was at hand even at the doors," were mistaken. All who have set the date of Christ's second advent, from that day to the present, have been mistaken. Irenaeus, a disciple of Polycarp, who saw and conversed with the apostles themselves, set the date five hundred years after the birth of Christ. Hippolytus, bishop of Portus, his disciple, wrote a commentary on Daniel and the Apocalypse, near the close of the second century, to allay the *panic* caused by a Christian writer named Judas, who attempted to prove from the Revelation, that the world would be destroyed in the tenth year of the emperor Severus. Hippolytus carried forward the date three hundred years; but both were in error. Some men of profound research have applied the prophetic language usually referred to the destruction of *papal Rome*, to that of *heathen Rome*; others have applied it to the destruction of Jerusalem. Amid such diversity of interpretation, whom shall we follow? We see that the elements on which any hypothesis respecting the future is based, are very vague and uncertain. The critics themselves are not inspired. They follow others who have stumbled and fallen. They reproduce their exploded heresies and support them by the identical arguments which their authors first used. They apply to our age the same threatenings which Christian writers of the first centuries applied to their times. Nothing is changed but the date. The exact time when prophecies in past ages were fulfilled, is still in doubt. What presumption is it, then, to dogmatize respecting those which remain to be fulfilled! If the beginning and end of "the seventy weeks" of Daniel is still a matter of controversy, why should we look for mathematical certainty respecting the twelve hundred and sixty days of anti-Christian rule? If it is difficult to determine with precision the *terminus a quo* of the four hundred and twenty years of Israel's bondage, or of the seventy years of the Babylonish captivity; *à fortiori*, will it be still more difficult to ascertain the point of departure for prophetic numbers in the future history of the world. The conflicting opinions of those who have made the attempt, in all past ages, confirms this assertion. If we should stand by a rapid river and see men attempting every day to ford it, and all, without exception, swept away by the current, should we not be deemed *insane* to follow them? Standing beside the mighty tide of human opinion, and seeing thousands sink in succession, may not that man be pronounced *insane* who boldly ventures to breast its swelling surges alone? It is asserted that the pre-millennial advent of Christ is a doctrine of the church in all ages, like the atonement. If so, why has it not been incorporated in any creed or confession of faith from the apostles' creed to the articles of belief adopted by the last church that has been organized in protestant christendom? In truth, it has never been deemed important except by those who, like the mistaken Thessalonians, were "shaken and troubled in mind" because they believed that "the day of Christ was at hand." On the contrary,

IV. When tested by the universal belief of the church, it is found to be "another Gospel."

1. The church, in all ages, has believed that the rest that remaineth for God's people was *in heaven;* that their glorious inheritance was reserved *in heaven;* that the "place" which Christ went before to prepare for his disciples, in his Father's house, was *in heaven.* According to the views of millenarians, the saints never enter heaven at all. They are reserved in "an intermediate state," till the resurrection, when they commence a reign with Christ on earth, which is to endure through "eternal ages."

2. It has been believed, *semper ubique et ab omnibus,* that the church would be absolutely complete at Christ's coming. The millenarians hold that by far the largest portion of it will be gathered in during the millennial reign; and that men in the flesh will live on the earth forever, who will also become subjects of Divine grace.

3. The church has believed in all ages that there would be a simultaneous resurrection of the dead, both of the just and the unjust. The millenarians maintain that there will be two resurrections, one at the beginning and the other at the close of the three hundred and sixty thousand years of Christ's earthly reign. "The hour is coming," said the Saviour, "when they that are in their graves shall hear the voice of the Son of man and come forth, they that have done good, to the resurrection of life, and they that have done evil, to the resurrection of damnation." The word "*hour*" frequently occurs in the discourses of Christ, usually designating a particular point of time. Here the millenarians bisect it, calling the beginning the *morning,* and the end the *evening,* of the resurrection, and inserting three hundred and sixty thousand years

between the initial and final terminus. If other books were so interpreted, what confusion would follow!

4. The church has ever associated the end of the world and the final judgment of the quick and the dead with the coming of Christ. They have believed the words of Paul in their natural import: "We must *all* appear before the judgment seat of Christ;" "he hath appointed a *day* in which he will judge the world in righteousness." According to millenarians, no such great day of assize will ever be known. The righteous dead will be raised at the coming of Christ and at once exalted to thrones in the new kingdom. The wicked dead will be raised at the close of the millennium and sentenced to eternal banishment. If geologists should so interpret the "days" of creation, these same men would shout "infidelity!" till they were hoarse. In the twenty-fifth chapter of Matthew the Saviour says: "When the Son of man shall come in his glory and all the holy angels with him, then shall he sit upon the throne of his glory; and before him shall be gathered *all* nations." Millenarians refer this passage to the nations that are alive at Christ's coming. It is the judgment of the "quick" and not of the dead. And, what is still more remarkable, these nations are to be judged by representatives or deputies. It is not expected that all the individuals that constitute the respective nations then alive will be summoned before the Son of man, but only multitudes or large numbers of them. Thus says Mr. Winthrop: "And before him shall be gathered all *the nations* ($\pi \acute{a} \nu \tau a$ $\tau \grave{a}$ $\check{\epsilon} \vartheta \nu \eta$) — that is, those who might be considered as in some respects representing all the nations." After arguing that many from infancy or other causes could not have had access to the sick, the naked, the hungry, and the imprisoned, and of course could not be included in either class then judged, he adds: "It follows, therefore, that those who are designated as 'the sheep and the goats' will *by no means* include *all the individuals* of the nations living upon earth at the epoch of Christ's second coming; and hence the parable furnishes no evidence against the fact in question."* Such logic is worthy of the acumen of Lord Peter in Swift's "Tale of a Tub." The great assize is converted by it into a mere temporal discrimination of the present inhabitants of the earth; and, with a little more pruning, might apply to the issue of the terrible conflict now raging between the great Western powers and the Czar of Russia. Mr. Dallas, an English commentator, is still more extravagant. He affirms that "all nations" means "all the *Gentiles*," and that the "sheep" are those who will be reserved to be the subjects of the glorified saints; and when Christ says, "come ye blessed inherit the king-

---

* Winthrop's Premium Essay, p. 144.

dom," it means "inherit the sovereignty described in the first chapter of Genesis — 'have dominion over the fish of the sea,' etc. *They are set apart as a new stock of the generation of Adam, whom he will educate for a thousand years,* without the influence of the devil to counteract the effect of a dispensation of sight." With regard to the "goats," he leaves the impression that they are "condemned;" but, as the time is not specified, it is probably at the final "sifting" of the nations at the close of the millennium! Thus "the end of all things" is not the end of anything in particular, but the beginning of many things in general; and the awful scenes of the last day,

> "Terror and glory joined in their extremes;
> Our God in grandeur and our world on fire,"

are softened down to the providential selection of his "sheep" by the "gentle Shepherd," from the nations then alive, at his second coming! Such conclusions, too, are reached by those who interpret the Bible *literally.*

5. The church universal has believed that the nations of the earth were to be converted before the second advent of the Saviour. Christ said as he was about to leave the earth: "Go ye, therefore, and teach all nations;" that is, make disciples of them, "and lo I am with you always even unto the end of the world," intimating that the Gospel should be successful among all nations before the end of the age. For this result, apostles, saints, martyrs and missionaries have labored; and, in their trials, toils and sufferings, they have been cheered with the hope that the Gospel would ultimately triumph. Millenarians teach that these views are fallacious; that the anti-Christian nations are to be destroyed, not converted; that the Gospel is to be preached as a witness apparently to ensure their condemnation rather than their reformation, and that our missionary plans are visionary and destined to disappointment. They say that missionaries should be sent in order to hasten on the glorious kingdom, and bring more speedily the advent of the blessed Redeemer, as if, forsooth, "the end of the age" were a movable period like some of the feasts in the church calendar. In fine, there is not a single doctrine of the Bible that is not essentially modified by premillennial speculators. They invert new "laws" of interpretation and thereby find confirmation of old errors. They use the Sacred Scriptures precisely as the Greeks and Romans did their Sibylline books. They quote by sound and interpret by feeling. The system of Christian theology seems to have suffered from internal convulsions similar to those which mark the geological epochs in the physical earth. Its strata

are dislocated, upheaved and tilted over, so that the inferior are often found cropping out at the surface or overlying the superior. No truth is *in situ;* but each must be referred to its proper "age" by an expert in pre-millennial hermeneutics. We are kindly informed that those who think the kingdom of Christ already established, "mistake the means for the end, and substitute what may be considered as a preparation for the kingdom for the establishment and manifestation of it." The pre-millennial theory is based chiefly upon the symbolic and prophetic portions of Scripture on which, in accordance with an old theological maxim, doctrines are not to be founded. "Theologia prophetica non est argumentativa." There exists great diversity of temperament, taste and opinion among millenarians. Some advocate our Lord's immediate appearing because they hope for it, love it, long for it, and *watch* for it. They are men who are full of Christian charity, who are by no means weary of duty on earth, but desire "to depart and be with Christ;" or, in their own language, to have Christ come and be with them. Others are restless spirits, who take pleasure in controversy, and desire a new economy that they may have a voice in the management of it. Knowing the future so much better than others, they seem to expect that superior attainments will command a corresponding position. Others are fond of the mysterious, the grand, and gloomy. With Sir Thomas Brown, they agree that there are not mysteries enough in the Bible to satisfy their active faith. They dwell so long in the valley of vision that they lose sight of sun and stars; then their thick-coming fancies overpower them, for nothing fills the eye like darkness. They make to the world wild and startling disclosures. They use the terrific language of prophecy to communicate their own dreams; and they sometimes mistake the reverberations of their own rhetoric for apocalyptic voices and thunderings. They dramatize the prophecies. The beasts and dragons of Revelation are made to play an important roll upon their ideal stage. They deal so much with the "living agents" of prophetic language, that their heads are as full of four-footed beasts and creeping things as the vessel that was let down out of heaven before the Apostle in vision; and their discourses are rather conversant with biblical zoology than with religious truth.

V. The moral influence of this doctrine is decidedly pernicious.

The best authorities assure us that it was attended, in the early ages of the church, with disorder and fanaticism. On this point, testimony has been already adduced. Whenever it has been agitated, in later times, it has always borne the same bitter fruit. It was never known to be productive of any good. It was a prevailing belief, in the Middle Ages, that the thousandth year from the nativity would usher in the end of the world. As the hour approached, signs and wonders were multiplied. Miracles abounded. On the heavens above were written tokens of coming wrath. The sun shone with a sickly hue. The moon refused to give her light. Strange voices were heard proclaiming "wo" to the nations. Apparitions and visions disturbed all classes. The monk at his vigils, the prisoner in his dungeon, and the serf at his task, all saw omens of approaching ruin. The devil walked in open day. Wizards and witches, prophets and magicians were multiplied. Terrible calamities fell on men and nations. Wars and rumors of wars disturbed all classes. Misfortunes thickened. The very elements seemed to sympathize with the fevered state of the public mind. The fruits of the earth were blasted. Pestilence and famine stalked through the lands. Terror drove the multitudes to fasts, vigils, and prayers. The roads were thronged with pilgrims. The churches were crowded to suffocation. The victims of disease and hunger died in the attitude of worship. The common feeling was, it is better to fall into the hands of God than to await his judgments. The rich bequeathed their wealth to the church, introducing their bequests with the solemn declaration: "The end of the world draweth nigh." Every class of society were smitten with terror, and trembled in agonizing apprehension of coming woes. But the fatal day came and passed, and the earth still rolled on as before. "The seed of the doctrine of gross Chiliasm has always remained in the Christian church. It has shown itself in various forms, and been taught in a more or less visionary manner. At the time of the Reformation, this belief was revived and widely spread by the enthusiastic Anabaptists, Thomas Münzer and his associates. They wished to establish this kingdom of Christ with fire and sword, and to put an end to all earthly power. Hence Luther and Melanchthon set themselves against this doctrine with great earnestness."* Calvin, too, speaking of the millenarians, says: "Their fiction is too puerile to require or deserve refutation." The fifth-monarchy men in Cromwell's time held the same notions. They believed in no king but Jesus, and proclaimed his immediate coming to judge the world. They set at defiance all law, and the sword devoured them. The followers of Edward Irving gave great celebrity to their pre-millennial views in England about thirty years ago. They owed their success to the genius and eloquence of their leader. All the miracles of the apostolic age were revived; and they succeeded so well in speaking with tongues that they almost deceived the very elect. Good men looked on in wonder, and doubted whereunto the thing would grow. But the light was a mere *ignis fatuus*, and when left to

* Knapp's Theology, Vol. II. p. 636.

itself it expired. More recently an illiterate farmer in Vermont studied the "sacred arithmetic" and announced the end of the world in 1843. Multitudes were alarmed by the apparent accuracy of his computations. Churches were divided, families were broken up, and our insane asylums were filled with lunatics. This moral epidemic did not cease when the predicted day had passed. The deluded followers of Miller still renew the date, and disturb the peace of the community with their pestilent heresy. They are denounced as fanatics and impostors by men who commend the works of Dr. Cumming as containing valuable religious instruction. Dr. Cumming uses the same data, and bases his calculations on the same symbols and numbers employed by Miller. The only difference between them is, that Dr. Cumming places the date of the coming of Christ a little later than his predecessor did. They are both of the same school; they preach the same doctrines and are obnoxious to the same charge of trifling with the dearest interests of men. Dr. Cumming not only predicts terrible judgments upon the nations, but affirms that present commotions are "the beginning of the end." "The stone cut out without hands" is now rolling. Many European nations have already felt the shock, and have reeled under it as from the rocking of an earthquake. These contributions to a general panic were presented in 1848. Had the prophet followed the advice of Horace,

———"nonumque prematur in annum,"

he would not have incurred, at once, the censure which falls upon the false prophet and the alarmist. But some birds can see best in the dark; others fly only in a storm; the former make night hideous with their hootings; the latter add to the terrors of the tempest by their unearthly screams. The modern prophet combines the characteristics of both. When the political heavens gather blackness, he is on the wing. When the night of misfortune broods over a nation, his voice is heard presaging ills. Big with conceit he comes as the herald of an angry God, to proclaim to a guilty world its approaching doom. His mission is to increase the excitement which ever attends national calamities; to give intensity to despair, and pronounce the bow of hope forever dissolved. The clouds are big with wrath; no mercy shines behind them. The sun has hid his face in impenetrable gloom and no bright future remains for the age. The dark forebodings of a gloomy imagination colors the dreadful picture. The awful language of inspiration is chosen to portray coming desolations. The majority of the ancient prophets lived in a declining and corrupt age; they addressed an apostate people; they were the heralds of coming woes to their nation; their messages were grand, gloomy, and peculiar. The Jews were the "chosen" depositaries of God's revealed will. The prophets were his "inspired" ambassadors. Such relations can never exist again. The condition of no nation can be precisely analogous to that of the Israelites. Modern prophets have nothing of the inspiration of ancient seers but their language; and, the more dark and enigmatical this is, the better will it answer their purpose of immediate effect. They have taken their position and they must maintain it. They have predicted that "the end of the world is at hand," and they must prove it. Where the signs of the times cannot be enlisted, as witnesses, they have recourse to exaggeration and bold and startling assertions. In this new Pandora's box which they have opened, no hope for the doomed millions now living lingers at the bottom. The elect are already gathered in; the last seal has been broken; the last trumpet has been sounded, and the last vial has been poured out, and the accumulated woes portended by these symbols are now rolling, like billows, over the earth. The end *must* come, do what we may; it cannot be delayed. The chariot wheels of the "King of kings" are now moving on the highway to fearful judgments. The wrath of God will burn to the lowest hell. The Gospel has been preached "*as a witness,*" and failed to convince the world of sin; now, it must prove a savor of death unto death to all that live; still the ministers of Christ must preach though they know that their labor in the Lord will be in vain, and that their efforts to enlighten their flocks will only enhance their condemnation and misery throughout eternity. Such busy speculators live in a continual fever. Their eyes, like telescopes, bring distant objects near, and magnify those that are at hand. Their ears, like hearing trumpets, catch the secret whispers of coming events and gather them to a focus, so as to render them audible to the unpractised multitude. At every dawning day, they are ready to cry out with Lenox in Macbeth:—

> "The night has been unruly: Where we lay,
> Our chimneys were blown down: and, as they say,
> Lamentings heard i' the air; strange screams of death;
> And prophesying, with accents terrible,
> Of dire combustion, and confus'd events,
> New hatch'd to the woful time. The obscure bird
> Clamor'd the livelong night: some say, the earth
> Was feverous, and did shake."

"I see," says Dr. Cumming, "the shadows of a dark night already forecast upon the world; I see dark and ominous shadows creeping, like birds of night, from every point of the horizon, all giving tokens of an approaching storm, that will rend and split Europe into fragments. We may, very speedly, have to witness men's souls looking with fear for the things that are coming upon the earth."* The evidences adduced in proof of this bold assertion are the revolutions then taking place in Europe, the eruption of Vesuvius in 1850, and an accompanying earthquake, the potato blight, the cholera, the increase of popery, and the increase of knowledge. Strange to say, a theorist can extract poison from the sweetest flowers of life. "Another sign of the advent of Christ," says the Reverend seer, "will be the spread of knowledge. Daniel gives this indication when he says : 'Many shall run to and fro and knowledge shall be increased.' Do we not see the signs of this around us?" Then he proceeds to enumerate the evidences of Satanic agency, to wit, the discoveries in science and art, the use of steam and electricity in social intercourse, the exploring of the depth of ocean and the caves of mountains, together with the godless speculations of philosophers.† But such things have occurred before. The world has always been slowly progressing in knowledge, and has always been subjected to physical and social evils. The reading of any child's history might have convinced the critic that calamities are not peculiar to this age. Every year since the birth of Christ the alarmist might exclaim with the utmost truth :—

"War, Famine, Pest, Storm and Fire,
Intestine broils, *Oppression*, with her heart
Wrapt up in triple brass, besiege mankind."

Such testimony in favor of any theory is utterly worthless. Some men seem to think that discoursing about the kingdom of heaven indicates a nearness to it; hence they substitute speculations about the future age, for efficient effort during the present age. Commentaries on the Apocalypse always abound in periods of religious declension. They affect the spiritual system as artificial stimulants do the physical. Revivals of religion have for the last thirty years been so few, that even good men begin to despair of the efficacy of the Gospel, and are looking for a miraculous interposition of the Saviour. They have become weary of waiting for sinners to repent, and they imagine that heaven must sympathize with their impatience. They comfort themselves with the hope of a restored earth and a new dispensation. But unbelievers may well say, in the language of tragedy :—

———"Of comfort no man speak,
Let's talk of graves, and worms, and epitaphs,

* Apocalyptic Sketches, First Series, p. 488. † Ib., p. 495.

> Make dust our paper, and with rainy eyes
> Write sorrow on the bosom of the earth."

The influence of such a belief is highly prejudicial to the spiritual welfare both of pastors and people. It leads them to undervalue the ordinary means of grace, and to withdraw from the benevolent operations of the day. It destroys hope. No man can labor who knows that he must labor in vain. Those who believe that the day of the Lord is "*at the very doors*," cannot engage in missionary enterprises with hearty earnestness, because that would imply the expectation of a remote future for this world. They feel much as the elder Adams did, when near the close of life. To a friend, inquiring for his health, he said, in substance: "This mortal tenement is very much shattered and disordered; and, as near as I can learn, the Landlord does not intend to repair." Such is the view which the pre-millennialists entertain of this disordered earth and its effete nations. It is soon to be burnt up and its inhabitants are to be destroyed (except a remnant) by the brightness of Christ's coming. For this they daily pray, whenever they repeat the petition, "thy kingdom come;" and they believe that "the effectual fervent prayer of the righteous man availeth much." If all believers in Christ should adopt the same views, and labor for the same results, within fifty years the church would become extinct.

Printed by Libri Plureos GmbH in Hamburg, Germany